DATE DUE

SEP 1 3	
JAN 3 0	
FEB 2 8	
JAN 1 1	
FEB 0 1	
FEB 1 2	
FEB 1 8	
Mar. 4	

Bill Gates

by Jonatha A. Brown

Reading consultant: Susan Nations, M.Ed., author/literacy coach/consultant

WEEKLY WR **READER®**
EARLY LEARNING LIBRARY

Please visit our web site at: www.earlyliteracy.cc
For a free color catalog describing Weekly Reader® Early Learning Library's list
of high-quality books, call 1-877-445-5824 (USA) or 1-800-387-3178 (Canada).
Weekly Reader® Early Learning Library's fax: (414) 336-0164.

Library of Congress Cataloging-in-Publication Data

Brown, Jonatha A.
    Bill Gates / by Jonatha A. Brown.
      p. cm. — (People to know)
    Includes bibliographical references and index.
    ISBN 0-8368-4310-X (lib. bdg.)
    ISBN 0-8368-4317-7 (softcover)
    1. Gates, Bill, 1955-—Juvenile literature. 2. Businessmen—United States—Biography—Juvenile
literature. 3. Computer software industry—United States—History—Juvenile literature. 4. Microsoft
Corporation—History—Juvenile literature. I. Title. II. People to know (Milwaukee, Wis.)
HD9696.63.U62G372 2004
338.7'610053'092—dc22
  [B]   2004044475

This edition first published in 2005 by
Weekly Reader® Early Learning Library
330 West Olive Street, Suite 100
Milwaukee, WI 53212 USA

Copyright © 2005 by Weekly Reader® Early Learning Library

Based on *Bill Gates* (Trailblazers of the Modern World series) by Lauren Lee
Editor: JoAnn Early Macken
Designer: Scott M. Krall
Picture researcher: Diane Laska-Swanke

Photo credits: Cover, title © Lynn Goldsmith/CORBIS; pp. 4, 14, 18 © AP/Wide World Photos;
p. 6 Courtesy of Lakeside School; pp. 7, 8 © Hulton Archive/Getty Images; p. 9 Computer Museum
of America; p. 11 © Deborah Feingold/Getty Images; p. 12 © Tim Crosby/Getty Images; p. 15 © Robert
Burroughs/Getty Images; p. 17 © Eriko Sugita/Reuters; p. 20 © Jeff Christensen/Getty Images

Printed in the United States of America

1 2 3 4 5 6 7 8 9 08 07 06 05 04

Table of Contents

Words that appear in the glossary are printed in **boldface** type the first time they occur in the text.

Chapter 1: Boyhood

Bill Gates has worked on many projects with his father.

Bill Gates was born in Seattle, Washington. It was October 28, 1955. Few people knew what a computer was. People wrote notes and letters by hand. Office workers typed on **typewriters**. At home, school, and work, life was different then.

Bill was a bright little boy who liked to read big books. He was good at math, too. In fact, he was always the best in his class at math.

Trouble in School

Even though Bill was smart, school was not easy for him. For one thing, he was the youngest kid in his class. He was small for his age, too, and he had big feet. Bill felt clumsy and shy. Even worse, he could not sit still. He tapped his fingers and jiggled his feet. It seemed that he never stopped moving. Sometimes he got in trouble for squirming so much.

After sixth grade, Bill went to a private school for boys. Some people said he was the smartest boy in school. But Bill did not make many friends there. He laughed at kids who were slow to answer questions. The boys he laughed at did not like Bill very much.

Bill watches his friend Paul Allen work on a new computer.

Although he made enemies, Bill made a few good friends. One was Paul Allen. They both liked working on a new machine at school. That machine was a computer.

Most computers were huge in those days. Those big, old computers were hard to use, too. But Bill and Paul didn't mind. They liked the challenge. They spent as many hours on the computer as they could. Soon the two boys knew more about using that computer than their teacher did.

Early computers were very large. They took up lots of space.

Chapter 2: College

Bill went to college at Harvard University.

Bill entered Harvard University in 1973. Harvard had a big computer. Bill liked that computer more than he liked some of his classes. He did not study very hard. Instead, he spent most of his time on the computer.

One day, Paul Allen brought Bill some big news. His news was about a company called MITS. MITS was making a computer kit. With that kit, people could build their own computers. They could have computers in their homes.

Bill and Paul were excited. They had talked and dreamed about this very thing! Now their dream might come true.

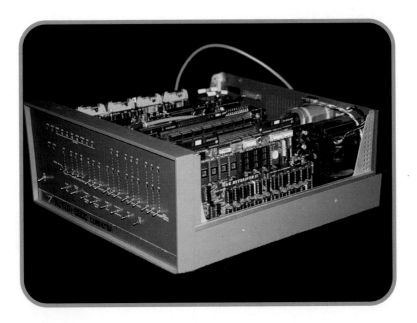

This is an old MITS computer.

The boys wanted to know more. They soon learned that the kit was not complete. It had no **operating system** — no brain to tell it how to work. It was really just a box with blinking lights.

Bill and Paul knew how to fix that problem. They would create an operating system to sell to MITS! The boys got to work. They hardly ate. They hardly slept. Day and night, they wrote **computer code**.

The First Sale

Weeks went by. The boys finished their work. They took the operating system to MITS. The head of the company watched it work. He said he would put it into his kits. Bill and Paul had made a sale!

A few months later, the boys took another big step. They set up their own company. They named it Microsoft. The year was 1975.

Bill and his friends started selling Windows in 1985.

All that time, Bill was still in college. His classes seemed boring to him. He did not want to be there. He wanted to sell operating systems. Finally, he left Harvard and did not go back.

Chapter 3: Microsoft

Microsoft is now based in Redmond, Washington.

At first, only Bill, Paul, and a few friends worked at Microsoft. They all wrote code for computer **programs**. They loved their work.

The group worked in New Mexico, where MITS was located. But Bill did not want to write programs only for MITS. He began selling programs to other computer companies. Bill did not want to stay in New Mexico, either. Paul agreed. In 1979, they moved Microsoft to Seattle. Bill was home again.

At that time, large companies owned most computers. They were not easy to operate. They took up a lot of space. They cost a lot of money.

Changing Times

A few years passed. The world of computers changed. More people learned to use them. Many wanted to have them in their offices. Some wanted to have them in their homes, too.

A company named IBM noticed the change. IBM decided to build a small computer. It would be just the right size for offices and homes. The people at

This IBM computer was small. It could fit on a desk.

IBM knew how to make the computer. But they had a problem. They did not know how to write the programs to make a small computer run.

They called Bill Gates. Could Microsoft write an operating system for the new computer? Could the job be done in a year? Bill said it could.

Now Bill and Paul had a problem. They had to write a huge program in a year! But they were smart. They solved their problem in a clever way.

Bill worked hard to make Microsoft a success.

They bought a program from another company. They planned to change that program. They would make it work on the IBM computer.

They still had a big, big job to do. Bill hired more people. They all worked harder than they had ever worked before. Finally, they finished the operating system. They named it Microsoft disk operating system, or MS-DOS.

Programs for Personal Computers

IBM soon started selling the new computers. They called them personal computers, or PCs. Millions of people bought them. And MS-DOS ran on every one!

Bill and his friends made a lot of money from MS-DOS. They used some of it to hire more workers. Then they wrote more programs. In a few years, Microsoft programs such as Windows, Word,

This boy is playing a Microsoft Xbox video game.

and Internet Explorer were running on PCs all over the world!

Chapter 4: Helping Others

Many years have passed since Bill and his friends wrote MS-DOS. Since then, Bill has continued to lead Microsoft. He has also made other dreams come true.

Melinda Gates works to help others.

One of his dreams was to have a family of his own. Bill met his wife, Melinda, at a company picnic. They were married in 1994. Melinda and Bill now have three children — Jennifer, Rory, and Phoebe. They all live in a huge house near Seattle.

Bill Gates is now the richest person in the world. He and Melinda can buy what they want. They also use some of their money to help others. They try to use that money in smart ways. They want to help solve big problems. Between 1997 and 2003, they gave more money to help others than anyone else in the United States.

Bill and Melinda give their money away through a **foundation**. The Bill and Melinda Gates Foundation has spent billions of dollars to help others.

Melinda Gates and Bill's father run the foundation. They travel around the world to see how they can help. Some money is spent for education. Some is used to buy computers for libraries.

Bill talks with women in India. He wants to help them and their children stay healthy.

Much of the money is spent on world health care. In some countries, millions of children get sick and die every year. Many die from diseases that could be

The Bill and Melinda Gates Foundation

The Bill and Melinda Gates Foundation gives money to four main kinds of programs.

Many programs try to improve children's health. Some give children **vaccines**. The vaccines help prevent serious illness.

Some programs work for education. They help high school students graduate and go to college. The foundation also gives **scholarships** to students.

Other programs give computers to libraries.

Some programs help people who live near Microsoft's offices.

prevented. Bill and Melinda want to wipe out those diseases. They want children all over the world to stay healthy. They are doing what they can to help.

Glossary

computer code — instructions for computers

foundation — an organization funded by donations. Many foundations spend money to help others.

operating system — a set of instructions that tells the parts of a computer how to work together

programs — sets of instructions (computer code) that tell a computer how to do different jobs

scholarships — money given to pay for education

typewriters — machines that print letters on paper

vaccines — medicines that protect against diseases

For More Information

Books

Bill Gates. Jeanne M. Lesinski (Lerner)

Bill Gates. Adam Woog (Kidhaven Press)

The Story of Microsoft. Adele Richardson (Smart Apple Media)

Web Sites

Bill Gates' House

papertoys.com/gates.htm

Make a paper model of the huge Gates home

Biography of Bill Gates

www.microsoft.com/billgates/bio.asp

Pictures of Bill Gates and information about his life and his work

Index

About the Author

Jonatha A. Brown has written several books for children. She lives in Phoenix, Arizona, with her husband and two dogs. If you happen to come by when she isn't at home working on a book, she's probably out riding or visiting with one of her horses. She may be gone for quite a while, so you'd better come back later.